To Eat Or Not To Eat?

The Vegetable Group – Food Pyramid (2nd Grade Science Series)

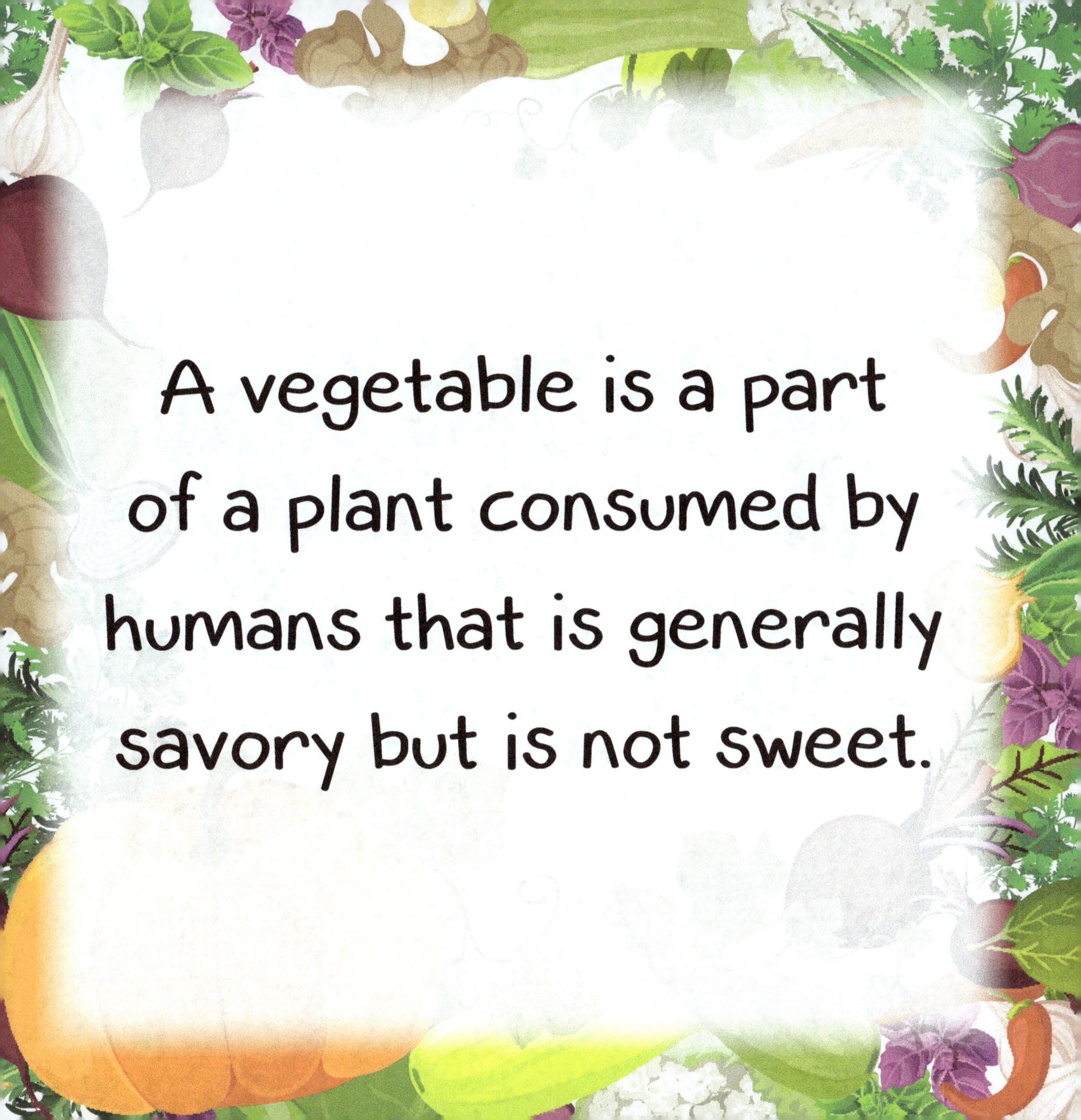
A vegetable is a part
of a plant consumed by
humans that is generally
savory but is not sweet.

Vegetables contain many vitamins and minerals; however, different vegetables contain different spreads, so it is important to eat a wide variety of types.

Vegetables are very low
in fats and calories,
but ingredients added in
preparation can often add these.

Vegetables

Frozen vegetables are just
as beneficial to the health
as fresh vegetables.

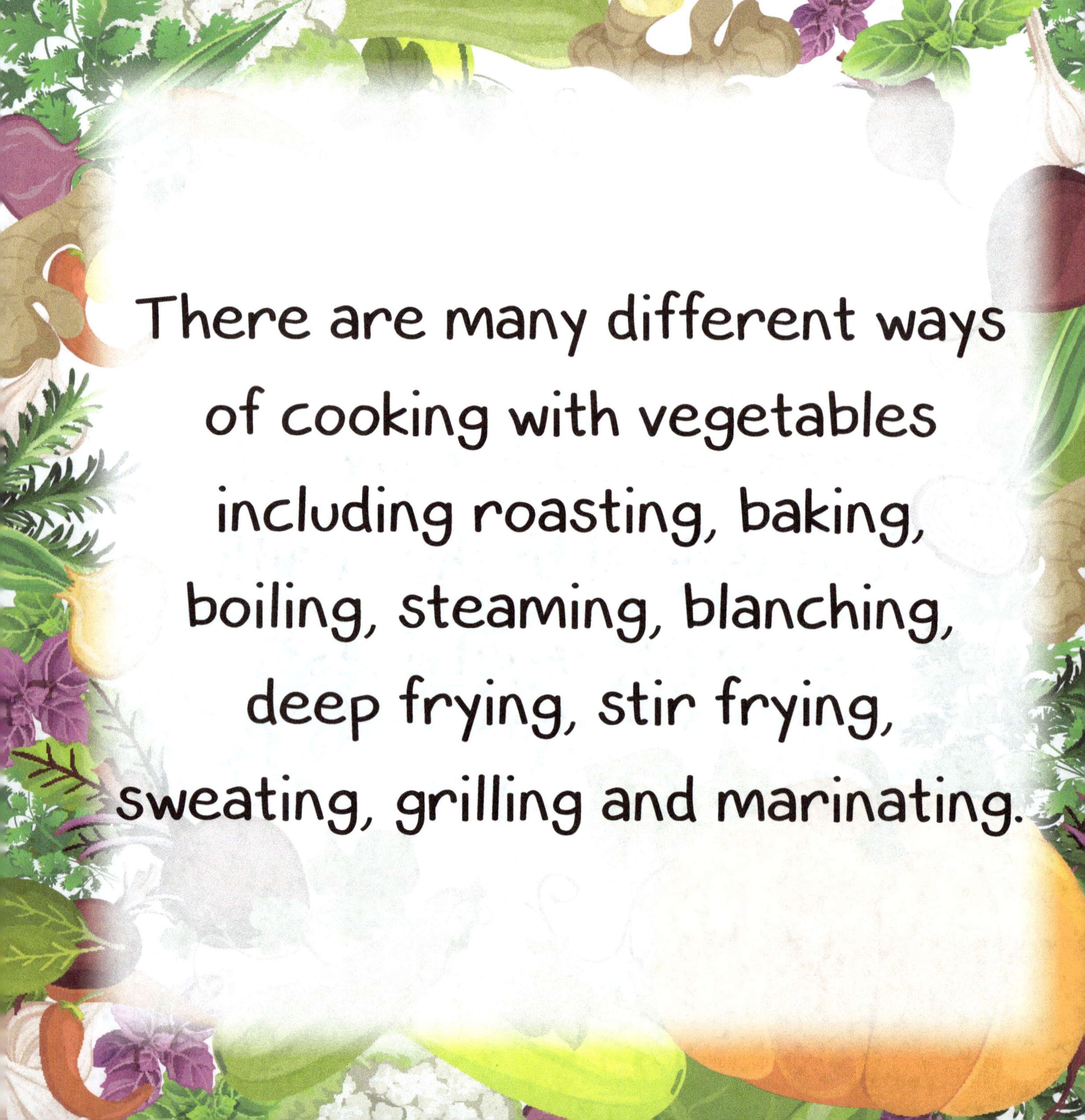

There are many different ways of cooking with vegetables including roasting, baking, boiling, steaming, blanching, deep frying, stir frying, sweating, grilling and marinating.

In the United States, more tomatoes are consumed than any other single fruit or vegetable!

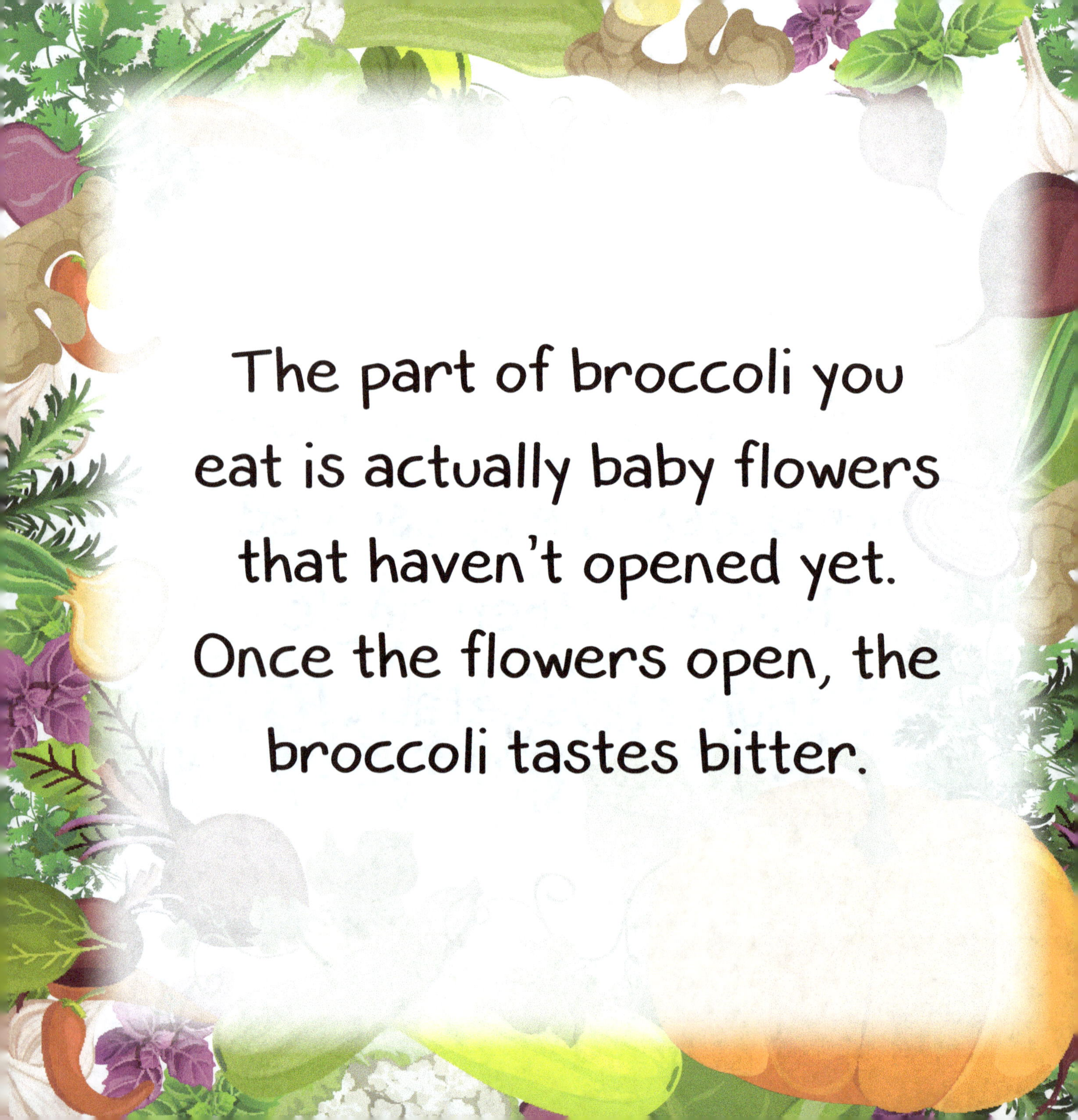

The part of broccoli you eat is actually baby flowers that haven't opened yet. Once the flowers open, the broccoli tastes bitter.

FRESH FROM THE FIELD
BEST PRICE

Vegetables come in all different sizes, shapes and colors such as green, purple, red and yellow, and they are grown specifically for food purposes.

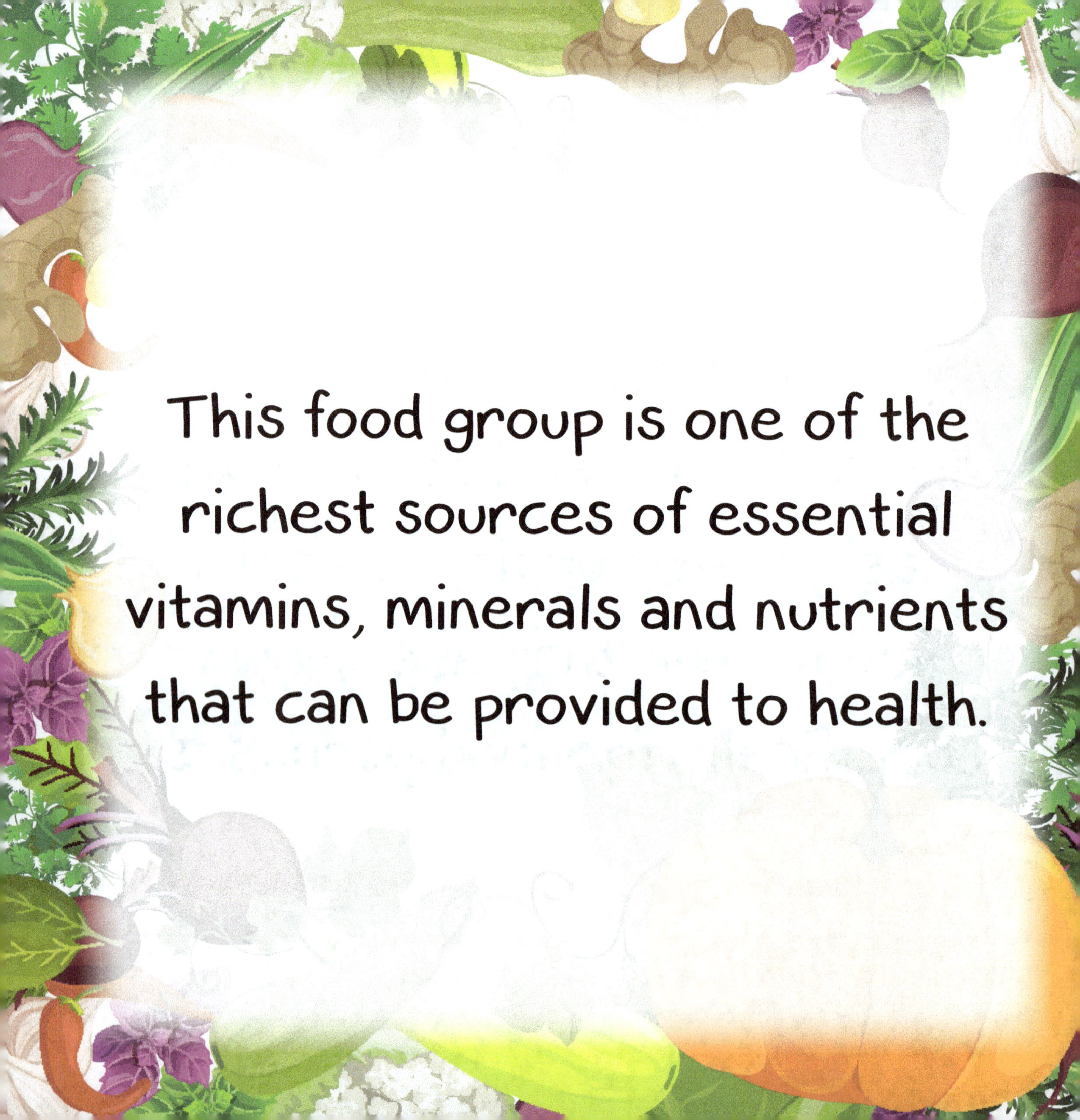

This food group is one of the richest sources of essential vitamins, minerals and nutrients that can be provided to health.

Vegetables can provide benefits to our skin, teeth, nails, hair and even help to prevent signs of ageing.

Green leafy vegetables are excellent for cooking as they are very versatile and can be cooked using many different methods including roasting, baking, stir frying, boiling, blanching and steaming.

Adding too much oil to
the roasting tray can
make vegetables soggy
& unappetizing.

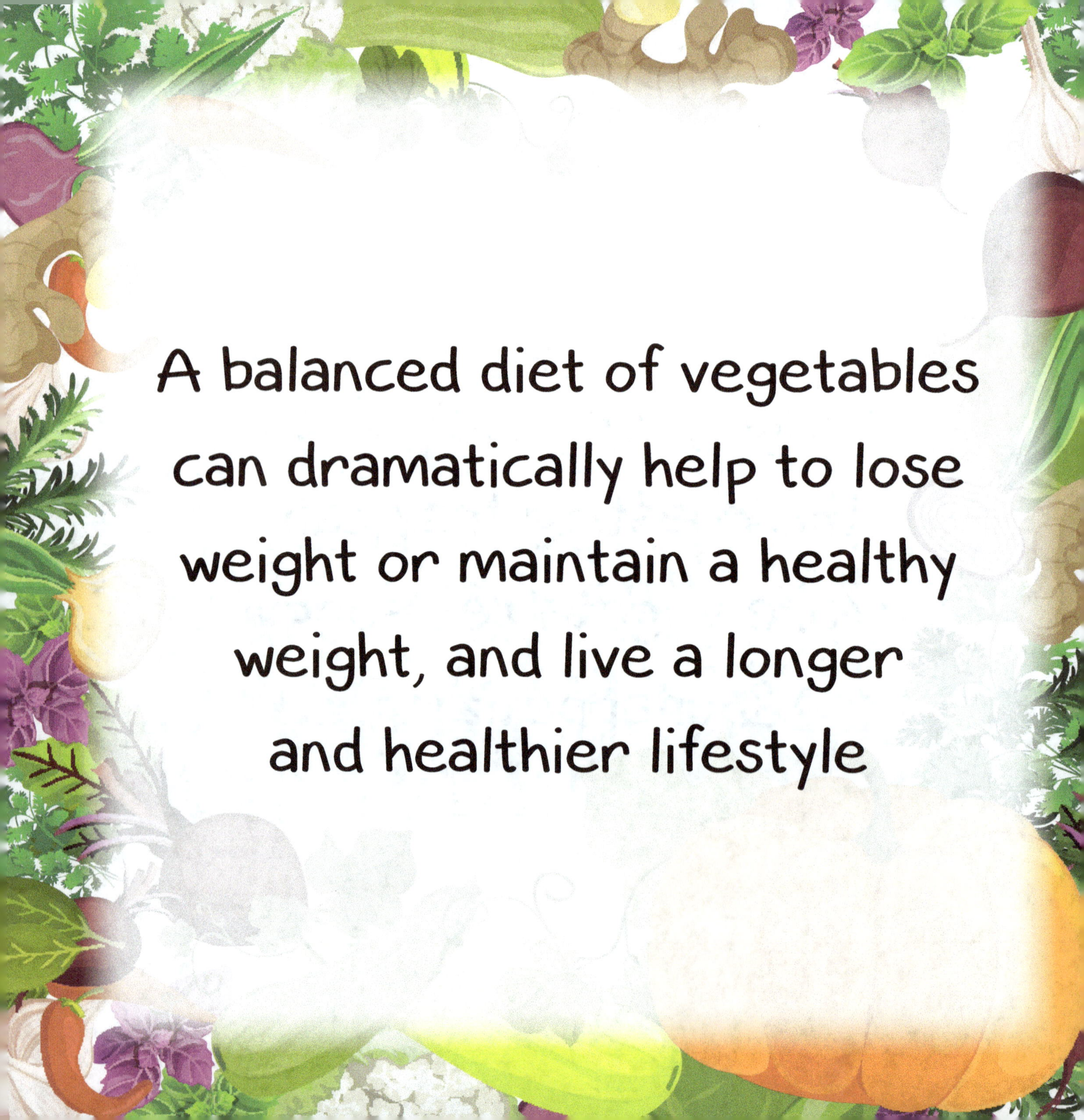

A balanced diet of vegetables can dramatically help to lose weight or maintain a healthy weight, and live a longer and healthier lifestyle

COLOR THE VEGETABLES

FIND 10

DIFFERENCES